Easy Jazzin' About

# Tangerine

Pam Wedgwood

2

# Easy Tiger

# Riding out west

## Smooth operator

# Let's get real!

# Hot chilli

## Crystal spring

# Keep truckin'

# Buttercup

**In waltz time** ♩ = 102

to Coda

D.S. 𝄋 al ⊕  **CODA**
poi al Coda

**poco rit.**

# Cat walk

# EASY JAZZIN' ABOUT
## fun pieces for
# DESCANT RECORDER

## CONTENTS

© 2004 by Faber Music Ltd
First published in 2004 by Faber Music Ltd
3 Queen Square London WC1N 3AU
Cover by Velladesign
Music processed by Don Sheppard
Printed in England by Caligraving Ltd
ISBN 0-571-52329-3

# PAM WEDGWOOD

**FABER ff MUSIC**

6.95

# Tangerine

Pam Wedgwood

# Dragonfly

# Easy tiger

# Riding out west

D.S. 𝄋 al 𝄌
poi al Coda

**CODA**

# Smooth operator

**With mystery** ♩ = 92

# Let's get real!

**More relaxed, with thought**

# Hot chilli

**With a Latin feel** ♩ = 132

# Crystal spring

# Keep truckin'

# Buttercup

# Cat walk